After reading Dorothy Williams's book of poems, I received illustrations of words that were pictured in my mind: inspirational words that were needed, love that was demonstrated as she was writing *Expressions from Deep Within*. I really enjoyed reading it.

Doris Bills

Expressions from Deep Within provides the reader with a vigor of emotions and imagination that awakens your soul. I truly enjoyed Dorothy's inspirations providing new perspectives for divergent situations.

Debra Dagen, registered nurse

Expressions from Deep Within is an inspiration to anyone who may be struggling through these hard times. Dorothy opened her heart and soul to all through her writings. I am especially proud of the words directed towards our teens. Life is often a struggle for them and it can be difficult to make the correct or appropriate decisions. Through her words, Dorothy lets us know that we are not alone. The words that she so eloquently wrote have helped me on many occasions to think about what is important and what is not important in life. Reading *Expressions from Deep Within* has enabled me to explore my expressions from deep within.

Gwendolyn Warren, LMSW

Expressions from Deep Within is one of the most amazing books I've ever read. It was really touching. I think that it would be helpful to anyone who reads it.

Laura Phelps

Dorothy did a nice job of interpreting God's words to comment on how we handle our everyday lives and hopefully to show us how to improve them. I especially liked "A Good Deed." It brought to mind a few people I know!

Deborah Smith-Olson, banker

Expressions from Deep Within has inspired me in many ways; from friendship to love, to family and to myself. Dorothy's words of the Lord make it easier for me to keep my faith in Him and myself.

Lisa Nickelson

Expressions from Deep Within is a great inspirational collaboration of poems. You will find yourself in many of Dorothy's poems and also learn from them. With many various poems ranging from spiritual life lessons and own personal emotions, readers of many ages will enjoy reading her writings.

Melanie Adkisson

Once I started reading *Expressions from Deep Within*, I could not stop until I read the entire book. I was impressed with Dorothy's creativity. It was very spiritually uplifting, as well as educational.

Lavern Stewart

I so enjoy Dorothy's poetry. She writes with such deep passions that the reader is allowed to look into her heart.

Linda Shively,
Shively Hewitt and Associates

In her book, "Expressions from Deep Within," the author, Dorothy Williams, understands life and emotions to a greater extent than most people. While reading it, there were certain moments when it tugged at my heart strings and made me feel her zest for life.

Kristie Stumbrie

"Expressions from Deep Within" is inspiring in many ways. It contains poetry that relates to life in the past, present and future, even the spiritual side. I think it would be beneficial to anyone who reads it.

Solomon Sims, Retired Minister

Dorothy has shown passion and deep feelings in "Expression from Deep Within." I felt peace, happiness and other emotions as I proceeded to read the entire book.

Marilyn Zdebski

Expressions
from
Deep Within

Dorothy Williams

Expressions from Deep Within

poetry

TATE PUBLISHING
AND ENTERPRISES, LLC

Expressions from Deep Within
Copyright © 2012 by Dorothy Williams. All rights reserved.

No part of this publication may be reproduced, stored in a retrieval system or transmitted in any way by any means, electronic, mechanical, photocopy, recording or otherwise without the prior permission of the author except as provided by USA copyright law.

The opinions expressed by the author are not necessarily those of Tate Publishing, LLC.

Published by Tate Publishing & Enterprises, LLC
127 E. Trade Center Terrace | Mustang, Oklahoma 73064 USA
1.888.361.9473 | www.tatepublishing.com

Tate Publishing is committed to excellence in the publishing industry. The company reflects the philosophy established by the founders, based on Psalm 68:11,
"The Lord gave the word and great was the company of those who published it."

Book design copyright © 2012 by Tate Publishing, LLC. All rights reserved.
Cover design by Jan Sunday Quilaquil
Interior design by Jomel Pepito

Published in the United States of America

ISBN: 978-1-62147-129-5
1. Poetry / Subjects & Themes / Inspirational & Religious
2. Poetry / General
12.11.14

Dedication

In dedication to
my children,
grandchildren, parents, siblings,
and my two aunts, with love.
Keep the faith!

Acknowledgments

First of all, I thank God for giving me life and for granting me the ability, as well as the opportunity to write this collection of poetry. Secondly, I want to thank Tate Publishing Company for accepting my work and making it possible for me to share my poetic artistry with many others. It is a great experience working with you.

I must thank all of my family members and friends who have supported my writings. Words can't express my appreciation for your love, support, and encouragement.

Special thanks to my friend, Martin Sr., for being such a wonderful friend. I will forever cherish your friendship, encouragement, support, and loving ways. I also want to give special thanks to LaTangie and Willie Sr. for their love, support, and encouragement.

I must acknowledge my late friend, Sarah, who stuck by my side until the very end. I will be forever grateful for all her support, encouragement, and inspiring ways.

Last, but not least, I want to thank my brothers and sisters through Christ Jesus and all others who have supported my poetic work of arts throughout the years. Your support and inspiring feedback did not go unnoticed. May God bless all of you!

Table of Contents

Introduction Poem	19
Let's Go There	20
A Beautiful Place	21
Give It Your Best	22
Take a Little Time	23
The Quality of Life	24
God's Concerns	25
God's Request	26
God Is Knocking	27
A Sinner's Plea	28
God's Reply	29
Pray for Peace	30
A Soldier's Prayer	31
The Cry of a Soldier	32
Prayer Changes Things	34
Share a Smile	35
Your Surroundings	36
I See His Work	37
Allow Me to Take You There	39

A Friend like You 40
Beauty Tip 41
A Lesson Well Taught 42
Cautious 43
Fair-Weather Friend 44
Living in Misery 46
Nutritious Thoughts 47
For the Sake of Peace 48
A Prayer for Mary Lou 49
Put It in God's Hand 50
Nutritious Thought 51
Helpful Tips 52
How 53
Prerequisites 54
Nutritious Thoughts 55
Taking You a Little Bit Higher 56
Something Is Seriously Wrong 57
Stop and Think 58
Mother and Son 60
Mary Lou's Confession (If only) 62
May God Bless Our Children 64
Nutritious Thoughts 65
Can't Stop Us Now 66

A Sinner's Prayer	67
God Answers Sinner's Prayer	69
The Wild Side of Life	70
A Change of Pace	71
The Prayer of a Preacher	72
One-Day Christian	74
Actions Speak So Much Louder Than Words	75
There Is No Need	76
Nutritious Thoughts	77
Slow Your Role	78
Settling Down	79
Choosing Your Mate	80
The Effect	81
Nutritious Thoughts	82
Seek for It	83
A New Way of Life	84
Work toward Your Goals	85
Never Stop Trying	86
Knowledge Is the Key	87
Let's Figure This One Out	88
Nutritious Thoughts	89
It's not time for us to quit,	90
My Dear Mother	91

Remembering the Times	92
God Is a Wonderful God	93
The Ultimate Test	94
What Would You Do?	95
In the Still of the Night	96
God Is My Salvation	98
Running this Race	99
Lend a Helping Hand	100
Why Are You Here?	101
Thinking of You	102
A Mansion of Love	103
Is It Really You?	104
Why I Love You	105
Loving You	106
Missing You	107
No One Knows	108
Take the Time to Express Yourself	109
My Request	110
Lord, I Need Your Help	111
A Prayer of Understanding	113
What God Will Do for You	114
Just Me, Myself, and I	115
God versus Satan	116

Reach for His Hand	117
Join Me in Prayer	118
A Prayer of Thanks	119
A Good Deed	120
My Lord, My Lord	121
As I Travel	122
The Power of His Love	123
Have Mercy, Lord	124
God Is the Way	125
Staying on the Right Track	126
As Children of God	127
Satan Will Try to Hold You Back	128
God's Word	129
God Is All of That	130
Let the Past Remain in the Past	131
Complain, Complain, Complain	132
Change Your Evil Ways	133
Teach Me, Lord	134
Nutricious Thoughts	135
The Extra Mile	136
I Have Found a Savior	137
I Have Been Blessed	138
Call on Jesus	139

Jesus, Jesus, Jesus	140
There Is No Need to Cry	142
It's Always Someone Else's Fault	143
Same Old Tune	144
God Is There Throughout the Season	145
Nutritious Thoughts	146
God's Mansion	147
Personal Poem	148
During Your Darkest Hours	149

Introduction Poem

Let me take you to a place,
Where you have never been.
To explore my expressions,
That come from deep within.

Let's Go There

Let's fly to the bright and beautiful sky,
No one else, just you and I.

Let's swim to the bottom of the ocean of love,
It's never too crowded not a push nor shove.

Let's sail to the island where harmony never ends,
And celebrate our unity once again.

Let's journey through the path of joy and peace,
To a land where happiness will never decease.

A Beautiful Place

There is a place I'd like to go,
Where joy and peace forever flow.
A place where bliss never ends,
And is pure from worldly sins.
Always calm and never dreary,
This is where I'd like to tarry.
This place is called paradise,
Cheerful, relaxing, and very nice.
So come with me, and bring your friends,
When this life comes to an end.

Give It Your Best

Give it your best, that's all you can do,
And always remain forever true.
Try not to react on every impulse,
You'll be amazed of the results.

Give it your best and keep on striving,
This is a key to continue surviving.
Although your work may slowly progress,
Just aim high; it will certainly manifest.

Give it your best and never give up,
Do not allow others to interrupt.
At times it may not seem to be enough,
Especially if the road appears to be tough.

We must be determined to do our best,
And not to worry about the rest.
Just be patient and give it some time,
At the end your work will shine.

If you give your very best,
This world will enhance north, south, east, and west.

Take a Little Time

Take some time for yourself,
Never place your needs upon a shelf.

Take some time to relax,
It's good for the soul, that's a fact.

Take some time to look around,
And listen to the lovely sounds.

Take some time to share an embrace,
It may elicit a smile on someone's face.

Take some time to speak a kind word,
It certainly will not go unheard.

Take some time to lend a hand,
To assist with whatever you can.

Take some time to kneel and pray,
You may encounter blessings along the way.

Take some time to rest your soul,
You'll be surprised what will unfold.

The Quality of Life

The car you drive may be far from fancy,
And your lifestyle may not be so jazzy.
You may live in a home that is not a mansion,
And the clothes you wear may not be of fashion.
Your neighborhood may not be the very best,
But always remember how much you are blessed.
The glasses you wear may not be expensive,
And you cannot meet the expense of contact lenses.
But God has blessed you, and it's all yours,
So don't worry about the things you cannot afford.
The shoes you wear may be very old,
But that's okay, because you have a soul.
Your soul is more important than all worldly goods,
And there's always good qualities in God's neighborhood.

Materialistic items are not important to God.

God's Concerns

God is not concerned about the length of your hair,
Nor is He interested in the clothes you wear.
He doesn't really care whether you're thick or thin,
But His interest is what lies deep within.

It really doesn't matter if you are a dignitary,
And it doesn't impress God that you may own a sanctuary.
His question is, did you extend a helping hand,
Or share His Word with a fellow man?

God is not interested in your fortune, or your fame,
Or whatever else you may have gained.
He's not concerned about the expensive meals you've eaten,
When he's more concerned about the
Children who are Beaten.

God is not concerned about your silver and gold,
A portion of His concern is on the many lost souls.
He doesn't care about your diamonds and pearls,
His main concern is what you have
done to enhance His world.

God's Request

Allow me to give your life a touch,
Of all the things you love so much.
I want to fulfill your every desire,
And take you just a little bit higher.
Allow me to dwell within your mind,
Sharing with you a very good time.
I'll take you high, and take you low,
Teaching you all that you'll need to know.
I'll fill your days with so much pleasure,
And happiness that is far beyond measure.

Allow God to control your life, not others.

God Is Knocking

God is knocking, please let Him in,
He wants to wash away your sins.
And grant to you the capacity,
To humble yourself so patiently.
God is knocking, please open the door,
His love for you, do not ignore.
He is trying to save your soul,
Please let Him in for His love to unfold.
Inside your mind, He wants to be,
Just let Him in and spend eternity.
With my Savior and dear Lord,
His presence here, you cannot avoid.
God is knocking, can't you hear?
He wants to keep you oh so near.
Just trust in Him and believe,
Eternal life, you will receive.

Allow God to purify your soul.

A Sinner's Plea

Lord, I'm here at the gate; please let me in,
I've been calling your name over and over again.
I thought you would keep this gate unlocked,
So there would be no need for me to knock.
My legs are tired, and my feet are aching,
My mouth is dry, and my body is shaking.
The road is bumpy and filled with stones,
But I'm here, Lord, to make this my home.
Please open the gate and let me come in,
I want to be free from all worldly sin.
I need for you to comfort me,
And nourish my soul eternally.

God's Reply

Who are you, and why are you here?
I thought for certain you didn't want me near.
Are you the person who refused to let me in,
To wash away your worldly sins?
It is much too late, you foolish child,
I waited on you for quite a while.
I have many others to tend to,
And I do not have the time for you.
I'm not concerned about your bumpy road,
Consider yourself blessed to still have toes.
The gate is closed permanently,
Because you've never found the time for me.
So turn around and go the opposite direction,
My child, it's far too late for my affection.

Tomorrow may be too late.

Pray for Peace

Pray for peace, this I say,
And God will protect you along the way.

Pray for peace here on earth,
A new way of life we shall give birth.

Pray for peace wherever we go,
God's holy words, we must know.

Pray for peace as we journey along,
With God on our side, we cannot go wrong.

Pray for peace, I do declare;
Trust in God, He's always there.

Pray for peace both night and day,
That harmony is here to stay.

Pray for peace for our solders in Iraq,
That God will safely bring them back.

A Soldier's Prayer

Father, upon your name I respectfully call,
Please lift my fellow soldiers if they shall fall.
I ask that you will protect me as well,
And lead us home safely, we have stories to tell.
Lord, we cannot fight this deadly battle alone,
And so many of our fallen soldiers have all gone.
Please be our shield as we fight,
And our shepherd throughout the night.
We need your love and helping hand,
To aid us as we so proudly stand.
In Jesus's name, I ask for your mercy,
As we proclaim our victory.

May God bless our soldiers.

The Cry of a Soldier

Soldier:
My God, my God, where are you?
My days are lonely, sad, and blue.
I've called on you from time to time,
You did not hear this cry of mine.
My God, my God, why aren't you near,
I need for you to erase my fear.
I thought you'd be close by my side,
Knowing I depend on you as my guide.

God's Reply:
My child, my child, where is your trust?
Believe in me; this is a must.
I always hear your humble cry,
And I would never pass you by.
I'm here for you, child of mine,
Just remember, I'm always on time.
Maybe not when you want me to,
But I've never turned my back on you.

Soldier:
My God, my God, I feel so ashamed,
You were always there when I called your name.
Forgive me, Lord, for not trusting you,
I should have known you'd pull me through.
I now understand your love for me,
And I'll cherish your affection endlessly.

God will never leave your side.

Prayer Changes Things

Say a prayer both day and night,
That everything will be all right.
Prayer certainly changes things,
You'll reap the serenity that it brings.
Prayer is the key to a relaxing mind,
It will carry you through the toughest time.
So take a little time to pray,
It will certainly brighten your day.

Share a Smile

Take the time to share a smile,
It may travel for many miles.

Share a smile with a stranger,
It may relieve all of his anger.

Take the time to share a smile,
And lift the spirit of a child.

Share a smile along the way,
It may brighten someone's day.

A smile can be highly contagious,
A frown can be so outrageous.

Your Surroundings

See the sun as it glows,
Feel the wind as it blows.

Hear the thunder as it roars,
On this earth as we toil.

Smell the freshness of the air,
The aroma lingering everywhere.

See the flowers as they bloom,
And the size of the moon.

See the lightning as it strikes,
Throughout the dawn's early light.

Watch the stars as they shine,
Through the shades and the blinds.

Stay in touch with your environment.

I See His Work

I see His work before my eyes,
Beneath the waters and in the skies.

I see His work shining through the sunlight,
And as it glows throughout the night.

I see His work surrounding me,
His incredible work, this I see.

I see His work in the vicinity of the county of Lake,
Every morning, I see His work as I awake.

I see His work in the trees,
Through the color of the leaves.

I see His work flying high,
Through the clouds in the sky.

What a lovely piece of art to see,
Demonstrating purity and serenity.

Enjoy the beauty surrounding you.

Allow Me to Take You There

Let's explore the facts of life,
The truth I will not sacrifice.
Relax your mind and let it flow,
I'm going for everything I know.
Taking it to the max this time,
Sharing all that's on my mind.

A Friend like You

I've shared with you my troubles now and then,
In you, I thought I had a friend.
You've rushed home to call your friend, Miss Sue,
And discussed everything I've shared with you.
You then contacted your close friend, Jan,
And started gossiping all over again.
You've always managed to call Miss Resa,
And had the audacity to contact Teresa.
You've stayed on the phone until about ten,
Gossiping with your other friends.
You've shared my troubles with Cousin Pat,
I had no idea you'd gossip like that.
My complete trust, I'd placed in you,
But gossiping is all you seem to do.
This must quickly come to an end,
I have yet to believe you are my friend.

This world is contaminated with busybodies.

Beauty Tip

Keeping your nose on your face
Will enhance your appearance.

A Lesson Well Taught

Too many times you've shared my business with Miss Sue,
I certainly don't need an enemy, with a friend like you.
You had the audacity to embarrass me
In the presence of Miss Jane,
I'm now convinced that you're surely insane.
My trust in you has come to an end,
I've finally realized that you are not a friend.
Grinning in my face has come to a halt,
This was a lesson that was very well taught.

There's a reason it's called my business.

Cautious

If by chance you hear me scream,
I'm just letting out some steam.
To avoid the massive explosion,
That may come from my emotions.
So take heed and disappear,
Because the time is drawing near.

The meaning of steam: Back off.

Fair-Weather Friend

When good news surfaced in the air,
It was certain that you were there.
But when bad news came around,
You were nowhere to be found.
A fair-weather friend, you are to me,
This did not take long for me to see.

When my spirit was filled with cheer,
I could always count on you to be near.
But when times were difficult for me to bear,
I found that you were never there.
A fair-weather friend you've proven to be,
When times got tough, you managed to flee.

When I needed a friend to talk to,
Where on earth were you?
You never bothered to come my way,
You disappeared for the entire day.
A fair-weather friend is what you are,
Whenever I was in need, you vanished so far.

When I was ill and needed a ride downtown,
You were again nowhere to be found.
By the time I became well, and able to help myself,
Our friendship was to the point where
There was nothing left.
A fair-weather friend I do not need,
When you come around, I must take heed.

A fair-weather friend is like having no friend at all.

Living in Misery

Each time a little joy comes your way,
You push it aside for a miserable day.
Whenever there's a chance for a day of laughter,
You focus on the bad times, including the day after.
There were times I have offered enjoyable things to do,
Your reactions were as though I'd thrown a brick at you.
You never look forward to having a moment of joy,
That may touch the heart of a little girl or boy.
Whenever the opportunity comes for a peace of mind,
You look the opposite direction each and every time.
I've often tried to share a pleasant conversation,
You always manage to cut it short, without hesitation.
I refuse to allow you to throw your sad life on me,
Just because you choose to live in misery.

Misery loves to accompany others.

Nutritious Thoughts

If you would stop
Trying to ruin my life,
And allow God to control yours,
This world would be a better place.

For the Sake of Peace

I often bite my tongue and tolerate your selfish acts,
You despise the lifestyles of many, but yours is not intact.
You don't seem to change, and you still refuse to quit,
For the sake of peace, I try hard to ignore it.

You're constantly throwing stones at everyone in sight,
Instead of lashing out, my tongue I continue to bite.
You refuse to analyze what you're doing to yourself,
For the sake of peace, I keep my thoughts to myself.

I try my very best, urging you to change your ways,
You look as though I'm crazy, and drift into a daze.
I often wonder why I tolerate your shortcomings,
But for the sake of peace, I ignore your grumbling.

I listen to your bickering and all your petty complaints,
You go as far as criticizing many of God's saints.
For the sake of peace, I try to understand,
But I have decided to put it in God's hand.

If I appear to be grouchy today,
It's because my tongue is sore from biting it.

A Prayer for Mary Lou

Lord, I come to you once again,
This time it is for Miss Sue's friend.
I really hate to bother you,
But I am so tired of Mary Lou.
She's trying her best to bring me down,
By slandering my name all around town.
She's worshiping Satan by doing his deeds,
And he's catering to her worldly needs.
Lord, I ask that you'd please touch her soul,
And if it's your will, please make her whole.
Please show Mary Lou a new way of life,
So that she may stop using her tongue as a knife.
She's cutting down everyone in sight,
I pray that you'll help her to see the light.
Lord, these terrible things are hard to ignore,
Because a lost soul, to me is a sore.
She often mistreats her friend, Miss Sue,
Lord, please have mercy on Mary Lou.
I know that she's lost in this sinful world,
I ask that you'll give her immoral life a twirl.

Say a prayer for those who persecute you.

Put It in God's Hand

If your enemies keep hanging around,
Trying their best to pull you down,
Pray that God will touch their hearts,
And to be your bodyguard.

If trouble appears to linger near,
And your world overflows with fear.
Put your matters in the hands of the Lord,
These things He will help you to avoid.

Nutritious Thought

Satan tarries in a sinful place,
God dwells in a clean environment.

Helpful Tips

It is impossible to judge the comfort
Level of someone's shoes,
If you have never walked in them.

You cannot compete in a marathon,
While choking on your feet.

It is unfeasible to be happy,
While dwelling in misery.

In order to be strong,
You must exercise your strength.

It is impossible to follow your dreams,
If you've never had any.

Never expect to be a winner,
While running with losers.

How

How can you reach your destination,
While sitting in the same spot?

How can you take care of your business,
While focusing on another's?

How can you remove the trash from another
Person's eyes,
If yours are filled with garbage?

How can you see a brick wall,
With your nose in the air?

How do you expect to achieve your goals,
If you don't work toward them?

How can you go forward,
While moving backward?

How can you speak,
With your mouth filled with garbage?

Prerequisites

If you want to succeed,
You must first give it a try.

In order to reach the top,
You must stop waddling at the bottom.

Before you attempt to save my soul,
You must first rescue yours.

If you want to lead,
You must know the directions.

Prior to loving someone else,
You must first love yourself.

Prior to being a hero,
You must have a challenge.

Before criticizing your neighbor,
Make certain your house is in order.

Before looking down on others,
Make sure you're someone to look up to.

Nutritious Thoughts

While you're butchering me with your tongue,
God is mending every part of me.

And while you're sowing your wild oats,
I'm planting seeds to enhance the beauty of this earth.

So it doesn't matter what you may think,
Or how you may feel about me.
There is a God who has accepted me as I am,
And is conditioning me to be who *He* wants me to be.

Taking You a Little Bit Higher

Allow me to take you in a different direction,
Because children need our affection.
I will not pull a single punch,
So prepare yourself and grab a lunch.

Something Is Seriously Wrong

Children are walking the streets at night,
Swearing, stealing, and initiating fights.
Some are drinking and using drugs,
Or finding someone who they can mug.
They're robbing stores left and right,
Coming home at daylight.
They do nothing but sleep all day long,
Because their parents are never home.
These children are throwing their lives away,
They do not have guidance, so they stray.
They're heading toward many hard times,
Because they must pay for their crimes.
Their parents are nowhere to be found,
They are out somewhere just hanging around.
They're either in a bar, or at a casino,
Not caring where their children may go.
Something is seriously wrong with this,
These children are certainly taking a risk.
Of being placed in a casket or in jail,
And some may land in a prison cell.

Children need our guidance.

Stop and Think

You get me out of bed before daybreak,
Let me rest a little longer, for peace's sake.
You drag me to McDonald's for a bite to eat,
Of course, I'm not hungry. I'm still asleep.
You take me to our neighbors' to play with my friend,
Because there's an important meeting, you must attend
When you finally pick me up, we go straight to McDonald's,
Is there something I should know about Mr. Ronald?
I'm hungry from all that playing I've done,
I gobble down a couple of burgers, one by one.
You rush home to watch the soaps you'd recorded all week,
This is the perfect opportunity for me to sleep.
Before I close my eyes, you're yelling my name,
I ask myself, "Is my mother insane?"
Why do I need to take the garbage out,
And why must she continue to yell and shout?
What is wrong with her two hands?
Boy! Some things I just don't understand.
Before I could crawl back in bed,
The phone rings, and it is Uncle Ted.
Now you want me to go to the store for your lazy brother,
This nonsense must quickly come to an end, Mother.
I wish I had the courage to say those things to her,
But my courageous mind is such a blur.

Now that the soaps are all over, it's dinnertime,
What is wrong with this mother of mine?
This really should be a major sin.
Ronald must be saying, "Here they come again."
Every day, this is what we repeat,
This is why my friends asked, "Is McDonald's
Your favorite place to eat?"
You had the audacity to say I'm obese,
And that my appetite needs to decrease.
How do you expect for me to become thinner,
When every day, you take me to McDonald's for dinner?
Maybe if you would cook a well-balanced meal,
I'd be much smaller, and you will save a few dollar bills.
Hopefully someday you will change your ways,
And I will have some peaceful days.
Can't you see what you're doing to me?
You're ruining my life constantly.

Mother and Son

Mother:
My child, why is it that every time I say Something to you,
It goes in one ear and bounces out of the other?
When I try spending time with you,
You say that you're on your way to visit with your brother.
Your father doesn't spend much time around the house,
And you spend so much time away from home.
I don't know what to do with myself,
I am beginning to feel so alone.

Son:
Mother, when I was willing to learn,
It was me that you refused to teach.
You said to gather my friends,
And go for a swim down at the beach.
I wanted to spend quality time with you,
But you stayed on the phone gossiping with Miss Sue.
When I requested to learn to drive a vehicle,
You told me to go outside and ride my bicycle.
You stayed on the phone so late at night,
And Dad left home to avoid a fight.
You pushed him away with your selfish ways,

I don't see how he stayed with you throughout the days.
Mother, now that I am fully grown,
I have a great life that does not keep me at home.
I'm spending quality time with my father,
And I often visit with my brother.
I'm sorry if you feel so alone,
But, dear Mother, you did this on your own.

Spend time with your loved ones before it is too late.

Mary Lou's Confession
(If only)

If only I had spent some time,
With this precious son of mine.
If only I had bonded with my son,
We could have had so much fun.

If only I had stayed off the phone,
My husband would still be at home.
I miss him oh so very much,
I really need his caring touch.

If only I had thought twice,
Before they drifted out of my life.
My husband and son mean so much to me,
Without them, I don't know where I would be.

If only I had shown them love,
We would be as tight as a hand in a glove.
I would not feel so trapped inside,
They'd be right here by my side.

If only I had prepared a decent meal,
So alone, I would not feel.
My days would not seem so long,
Where else did I manage to go wrong?

If only I had another chance,
My family life will certainly enhance.
I'd do all the things a mother should do,
And my faults as a wife would be very few.

Never take your loved ones for granted.

May God Bless Our Children

May God bless our children who do not have a home,
And those with parents who love to roam.

May God bless our children without food to eat,
And those who do not have shoes for their feet.

May God bless our children without clothes to wear,
And those who may have heavy loads to bear.

May God bless our children who are ill,
Heal them, Father, if it's your will.

May God bless our children who cannot talk,
And all those who may never learn to walk.

May God bless our children who have no one to love,
Please allow your mercy to pour from above.

Lift our children up in prayer.

Nutritious Thoughts

Children are precious gifts from God,
They are lost in this world, and need our guidance.

Can't Stop Us Now

We can't stop now; we're on a roll,
There are things that should be told.
We're stepping on toes left and right,
Please refrain from getting uptight.

A Sinner's Prayer

Lord, I come to you once again,
Because I may have committed a sin.
I may be wrong, and I need your mercy,
Please show a little compassion for me.
I partied all night, and I drank a little wine,
But I must confess, I had a great time.
Honeys were all over the place.
Did you observe the smile on my face?
Ladies were dressed in Daisy Dukes,
Their horns, I must sincerely toot.
I yelled, "Lord have mercy," each time they
Walked through the door,
To me, last night was certainly not a bore.
Miniskirts bounced all over the tables,
I found it difficult to remain stable.
Forgive me, Lord; I must speak the truth,
They kept me running to the drinking booth.
Ladies wore weave down their backs,
And some were dressed in the tightest slacks.
They appeared to have been heavenly sent,
Lord, please tell me why do I need to repent?
Tension was floating all in the air,

Brothers were mad, but I didn't care.
The party was jumping, and so was I,
It seemed as though time flew right by.
The dance floor was packed without a doubt,
I had the opportunity to scream and shout.
Lord, I will definitely go back for more,
To admire those women on the dance floor.
I jumped around all night long,
Partying hardy by every song.
I know you probably think that I'm insane,
But Lord, last night, I did not feel any pain.

Why ask for forgiveness, when you intend
To do the Same thing again?
God frowns on premeditated sin.

God Answers Sinner's Prayer

Why do you always call my name,
Playing your silly, pathetic games?
You indulge yourself in premeditated sin,
Whenever opportunity presents, you do it again.
You wouldn't know forgiveness, if it slapped you in the face,
Your wickedness is a total disgrace.
Why bother me, when you know you're not sincere?
Listen, my child, I must make this clear.
I don't have time for your foolish games,
Do you think I'm stupid? You *are* insane.
Stop wasting my time. I have better things to do,
When you are sincere, I will assist you.
There is one more thing that you must know,
You will definitely reap whatever you sow.

The Wild Side of Life

You dip and dab with Miss Sue,
And run around with Mary Lou.
You break every commandment God has given,
With the lifestyle you are living.

You often chase your neighbor's wife,
Knowing she lives a sinful life.
She has a husband of her own,
But chooses to go outside of her home.

Eventually this will come to an end,
Because God is frowning on your sins.

A Change of Pace

It's time for me to change my pace,
Ladies, wipe that smile from your face.
Some of you are as bad as the men,
Committing all those awful sins.
You appear to possess no self-pride,
Those lousy things you cannot hide.
You don't stand for anything, and will fall for it all,
Some men are out there just to have a ball.
Your outer appearance may appeal to a man,
But he's just out to get whatever he can.
Although they spread themselves around,
Men don't want what's been around town.
When they decide to choose their wives,
They do not want you in their lives.
So take some pride in yourself,
And store your goodies on the shelf.
Mr. Right will come along one day,
So believe these words that I say.

The Prayer of a Preacher

Lord, I came to this building to teach your Word,
I really don't think that I've been heard.
The members are constantly testing my faith,
I'm beginning to feel as though it's a waste.
They sit at the bars throughout the weekend,
And come to service smelling like gin.
Women strut through the door with Casanova,
And sit in the pews, with a hangover.
Most of them arrive extremely late,
Dragging their feet, with a headache.
We always start service after eleven,
They're in the choir singing, "Stairway to Heaven."
They snap their fingers and dance to the tune,
Lord, please do something very soon.
Father, why did you send me here to teach?
They really don't listen when I preach.
They blow bubble gum, as though it's okay,
And sit and snore each time I pray.
They pass around handkerchiefs for everyone to use,
Throughout the service, they're wiping their shoes.

Women are wearing their miniskirts,
And the guys wear Playboy symbols on their shirts.
Lord, I realize that I don't stand a chance,
Because their lifestyles will not enhance.
Dear Lord, I'm praying for your aid,
Because this nonsense will not fade.
I'm begging you, Lord, to hear my plea,
Those guys are keeping all the women from me.

Be careful who you choose as a leader.
If a sinner leads a sinner, they both will be lost.

One-Day Christian

Every Sunday morning you attend worship service,
You profess to be a Christian, and sing in the choir.
You jump around shouting, claiming
To have the Holy Ghost,
While falling over chairs, speaking in unknown languages.
The following Monday, you're up bright and early,
Thinking of ways to destroy your neighborhood.
You then count your money to do a little gambling.

Regardless of how much you sing and shout on Sunday,
And indulge in sinful behaviors Monday through Saturday,
It is not God that you seek,
Your soul is lost seven days a week.

It is impossible to be a Christian on Sunday,
While worshiping Satan throughout the week.

Actions Speak So Much Louder Than Words

You told her that you love her, this I have yet to see,
Just the other day, you tried flirting with Miss Bea.
Her vehicle had a flat tire and was sitting beside the road,
You said to call a wrecker, and to have it towed.
Today you said that you really do care,
But when she asked how much, this you refused to share.
How can you care for her, while doing the things you do,
And when you say you love her, you never speak the truth.
You really don't know the meaning of true love,
There's no way you can love her, as
much as you push and shove.
While lying in bed, sick for days,
The treatment she received, I was not amazed.
She asked if you would bring a bite to eat,
You prepared the food, then threw it on her feet.
She asked you for a cup of tea; you poured it in a saucer,
She really doesn't need those terrible things you offer.

There Is No Need

There is no need to fuss and fight,
And toss and turn throughout the night.
If it's impossible to get alone,
Don't waste your time, you should be gone.

There is no reason that you should not be elated,
All that confusion, you should just hate it.
Life is too short to live in misery,
Try to be as happy as you can be.

There is no need to endure the pain,
What on earth will you gain?
Do what you can to put it to a halt.
Use those strategies that you were taught.

Try to enjoy every moment of your life.

Nutritious Thoughts

You may never know what's floating inside of the head,
Of the one lying next to you in bed.
In some cases, it doesn't take long before love turns to hate,
So try and solve the problems before it's too late.

Slow Your Role

Slow your role before it's too late,
And take precaution for your own sake.
There's something out there that's hard to heal,
So think about it, if you will.
It's spreading around like wildfire,
And is something no one desires.
It does not possess sympathy,
And doesn't care who you may be.
It has taken many innocent souls,
So please take heed and slow your role.
No one has found joy in this,
It attacks your body and will not miss.
It lingers inside until the end,
So slow your role, my dear friend.
It attacks your mate with a fresh start.
And hangs around until death do you part.
It's not worth your precious life,
So slow your role and think twice.

HIV has a friend following him everywhere he goes.
His friend is called AIDS, and it has taken many souls.

Settling Down

After you've spread yourself around town,
You said that you wanted to settle down.
You had the audacity to ask for her hand,
Saying that it's time to become a real man.
Why would you think she'd marry someone like you,
Who possesses values that are very few.
With you, she must not waste her precious time,
Without a doubt, her soul mate, she will find.
Why should she settle for so much less,
Because she deserves the very best.
So go and marry someone like you,
Who does the things you always do.

Always aim for the best,
Never, ever settle for less.

Choosing Your Mate

Choose your mate wisely, and never settle for less,
Take your time and seek for the best.
We all have faults, and we're far from perfection,
Just be sure there's some type of connection.
Communication is definitely a must,
This will eliminate a great deal of fuss.
So take some time to get to know your mate,
And be cautious of those various baits.
Don't be overtaken by such smooth talk,
And never be afraid to say, "Take a walk."
Respect is the key to a healthy relationship,
Understanding should fall in place, and never flip.
Give your best and expect the same in return,
You'll be surprised of what you may learn.
Sometimes it may take a little longer,
For the relationship to grow stronger.
This can be a good thing at times,
Because you're cautious of the little signs.
Minor things may be overlooked,
But be sure you can deal with it before you're hooked.
The first sign of violence should not be ignored,
Let it go, and *never* get on board.

The Effect

You went to a party early last night,
Because you were so uptight.
Someone offered a glass of alcohol to you,
And you decided to have a drink or two.

You then went to the home of a friend,
And stayed over there until about ten.
With him, you shared all your troubles,
He said to you, "This calls for a double."

He said that your days would be much brighter,
Your friend then asked you for a lighter.
He lit up a pipe and took a hit,
He then offered you a little bit.

"This will make things better for you,
So help yourself to a hit or two."
This is what your friend had said,
Before you came back and found him dead.

Take heed if you will,
Because drugs just might kill.

Nutritious Thoughts

Teens experience peer pressure all the time,
It takes control of their innocent mines.
Take the time to show that you care,
Because temptation will always be there.

Seek for It

Whatever it is you want to obtain,
Seek for it, and this you will gain.

Whatever it is that's holding you back,
Kick it to the curve and give it no slack.

Whatever it is your heart desire,
Seek for it, and move a little higher.

There's nothing impossible for you to do.
Believe in yourself, your dreams will come true.

You will never grasp hold of it,
If you don't reach for it.

A New Way of Life

Look around and see what life has in store for you,
There are so many positive things for you to do.
Don't waste your time doing nothing at all,
Lift yourself up, and you will stand tall.

Take a look around to seek your calling,
Then jump right on it, no more stalling.
Many opportunities are preserved for you,
Challenge yourself to a life that's new.

Never be afraid to take a few chances,
You'll be surprised when your life enhances.
Always try to improve yourself,
You may encounter a little self-wealth.

Work toward Your Goals

Days are constantly going by, one by one,
But don't give up until your work is all done.
Keep moving forward until you succeed,
You'll reap a reward for your good deed.

Set your goals and work toward them,
Even if the path may seem a little dim.
With a little determination, you'll do your best,
And draw a little closer toward success.

Gather your tools and hold them tight,
Your reward will soon be in sight.
Don't allow anything to turn you around,
You'll soon place your feet on successful ground.

If by chance you encounter cloudy days,
Just remember, hard work always pays.
Never give up on accomplishing your goals,
You'll be surprise what the future will hold.

Never Stop Trying

In case you shall fail, give it another try,
A little more effort, you must apply.
Your effort will pave a broad road to success,
So make sure your goals include the very best.

Success is not always easy to obtain,
But once it is achieved, your life will not be the same.
So gather your knowledge and maneuver along,
Never give up, keep moving strong.

Learn your strength and work with it,
Be persistent, and do not quit.
Take a moment to contemplate,
And research your weakness, never hesitate.

You must then eliminate this from your plan,
Focus on your strength as much as you can.
Your strength is the key to your success,
This will definitely be manifested.

At times, things may seem a little difficult,
But keep on going, and never give up.

Knowledge Is the Key

Stay in school and learn all you can,
This will assist you, as you become a man.
This goes for all the females as well,
Do all you can to excel.

Sometimes it may take a little contemplation,
But never give up on a higher education.
Take it to the max, and you will be proud,
To walk across the stage, in front of a crowd.

Knowledge is a must, if you want to succeed,
Do your homework, and take time to read.
Always be prepared to pass a test,
Be good to yourself, and go for the best.

Learn as much as you possibly can,
On solid grounds, you shall land.

Let's Figure This One Out

How can you pay your bills without any money?
How can you earn money without a job?
How can you get a job without an education?
How can you get an education without learning?
How can you learn without paying attention?
How can you pay attention if you're constantly talking?
How can you enjoy life if you don't know anything about it?

How can you help someone if you can't help yourself?
How can you be proud of yourself if you don't have pride?
How can you live a peaceful life if you
Surround yourself with drama?
How can you not be corrupted if you waddle in corruption?
How can you be somebody if you're hanging with nobody?
How can you feel good about your accomplishments,
If you haven't accomplished anything?
Why didn't you learn when you had a teacher?
How can you allow anyone to mold you if
You insist on destroying your life?

Nutritious Thoughts

Education is something you will not live to regret,
This is something you should never forget.

*It's not time
for us to quit,
But let's slow
down a little bit.*

My Dear Mother

On my way to school, I think of you,
And the things you always do.
You wake up early to prepare my lunch,
Nutritious food, I have a bunch.
You wash my clothes and press them too,
I'm very proud to have a mother like you.
You always make sure my homework is done,
Before I begin to play and have a little fun.
Food is prepared when I arrive home,
You never, ever leave me there alone.
The sitter is always waiting for me,
To make sure I arrive home safely.
When you return from work each day,
You make sure that I'm okay.
You give a very warm embrace,
With a pleasant smile on your face.
You tuck me in bed and read to me,
You are as caring as can be.
When Dad comes home, walking through the door,
His hungry body, you do not ignore.
Dinner is always prepared on time,
I admire you so much, dear mother of mine.

Remembering the Times

Remembering the times you tucked me in,
And read to me all over again.
You stayed by my side until I fell asleep,
Those are the memories I'd like to keep.

I'll never forget those walks in the park,
And how we rushed home before it was dark.
We had so much fun, just you and I,
Pleasant days never passed us by.

I remember the time I flew a kite,
And the very first time I rode a bike.
You were always there to share my joy,
And never hesitated to give a toy.

I remember the time when I hurt my back.
Your tender loving care, I did not lack.
You stayed by my side until I recovered,
A parent like you, I'll never feel smothered.

Those are a few moments that we've shared,
And I'll never forget how much you care.
It is your precious, caring touch,
That will always mean so very much.

God Is a Wonderful God

God is truly a wonder God,
He has never committed a fraud.
But He can bring you to your knees,
Saying: please, please, Lord, please.
He wants you to do His divine will,
And your peace of mind, no other can steal.
God is wonderful to all of us,
Whatever we need, He'll grant without a fuss.
He will supply our necessary desires,
What a great God to admire.

The Ultimate Test

God separated a man from all the rest,
And sent him in your direction as a test.
To examine your soul from deep within,
But you failed the test once again.
When his soul was lost, you gave no directions,
But confused him more, without affection.

God sent this man to your home the following day,
To test your mind in another way.
He came to you hungry, and you fed him not,
You refused to share, although you had a lot.
You possessed a freezer packed with meat,
You still refused to share a bite to eat.

God tests us in many different ways!

What Would You Do?

Would you extend a helping hand,
Or
Would you rather point a finger?

Would you help your fellow man,
Or
Would you put him through a wringer?

Would you reach out to be a friend,
Or
Would you prefer to be left alone?

Would you be there until the end,
Or
Would this remain unknown?

In the Still of the Night

I came to your place in the still of the night,
There was not a spiritual trace in sight.
A picture of your loved ones was on a nightstand,
And hanging in the ceiling was a beautiful fan.
I took a look around and there I saw,
A gorgeous painting hanging from afar.
I went to the kitchen, and took a seat,
And admired the tile beneath my feet.
I walked to the family room, and was so amazed,
I sat on the couch; and there I gazed.
What a pleasant sight for one to see,
Oh, how I enjoyed every scenery.
It was so marvelous what I had seen,
Your place was in fact, tidy and clean.
I examined your home inside and out,
You're living extravagantly, that's no doubt.
But there was one thing I did not see,
There was not a sign of spirituality.

I thought to myself, "What would you do,"
If I decide to take this from you?
But I will certainly give you a chance,
To see if your lifestyle would soon enhance.

What would God see if He visits your home?
Give thanks for all you have,
Because if it wasn't for God, you would not have it.

God Is My Salvation

God is my one and only salvation,
He protects me from all worldly temptation.
I depend on Him every day,
To guide my steps so I will not stray.

God is my salvation, yes, indeed,
He's always there when I'm in need.
As I kneel to pray each day,
I thank the Lord for leading the way.

My salvation, God is to me,
He is as wonderful as can be.
He's my sister and my mother,
He's my friend, my father, and brother.

Running this Race

As I attempt to win this race,
I must maintain a steady pace.
I cannot be too early, not late,
But arrive on time to enter the gate.
I cannot afford to fail this test,
I'm giving this my very best.
I may encounter obstacles along the way,
But I'll keep on moving every day.
Until I reach my destination,
I'll run this race with jubilation.

Feel the power God has for you,
It will elicit peace in all you do.

Lend a Helping Hand

If I am sinking,
Don't give me weight.
Try lifting me up,
Before it's too late.

If you think that I'm in pain,
Don't kick me in my head.
But do whatever you can,
To ease my pain instead.

If I'm lost in sin,
And cannot find my way,
Show me how to save my soul,
And I may have a brighter day.

If by chance I shall stumble,
Please don't knock me down.
Help me to gain stability,
To keep my feet on the ground.

And if you see me falling,
Lend a helping hand.
God will smile on you,
And He'll help *you* to stand.

It does not hurt to go an extra mile.

Why Are You Here?

Are you here to criticize your neighbor,
Or
Are you here to extend a favor?

Are you here to fight with others,
Or
Are you here to make peace with your brother?

Are you here to destroy whatever you can,
Or
Are you here to build with your fellow man?

Thinking of You

I think of you every day,
At times these thoughts get in my way.
It's hard for them to disappear,
Oh how they always linger near.
I think of you every night,
And the times you've held me tight.
Thoughts of you will not erase,
They tarry near with a steady pace.
I think of the good times that we've shared,
And all the times you've shown you care.
Memories are hard to let go,
Throughout my mind, they always flow.
I think of you through thick and thin,
These thoughts will never come to an end.

A Mansion of Love

I've prepared for you a dwelling place,
The location is in my heart.
Nice and cozy with so much space,
No one can ever tear it apart.
It's a mansion of love that's coated with smiles,
The foundation is made of trust.
There's not a creature for many miles,
And never an ounce of dust.
It's violent proof, and not made to destroy,
Consideration and caring is always demanding.
It's laced with comfort and coated with joy,
Has a finishing touch of understanding.
This mansion is fenced with respect and love,
The environment will always enhance.
Many blessings will come from above,
To shine on our sacred romance.

Is It Really You?

Sitting here on my patio,
Listening to the sounds from my radio.
Watching the birds as they fly,
A glance of you catches my eye.
Having to take a second look,
One more glimpse was all it took.
For me to sit and gaze your way,
While searching for words to say.
Images of you are clouding my view,
Is it my imagination, or is it really you?

Why I Love You

I love you because your love is true,
I cherish each moment spent with you.

I love you because you rock my world,
When it was confused, you gave it a whirl.

I love you because you're heavenly sent,
You give me no reasons to repent.

I love you because you are unique,
With you in my life, no other I seek.

Loving You

I love you oh, so very much,
I love your tender, caring touch.
You've touched my heart more ways than one,
Being with you is so much fun.
You have a way of turning things around,
Never having to make a sound.
If these feeling are a crime,
I'm praying not to serve the time.
The jury may find me at fault,
Because I cannot put this to a halt.
The judge may sentence me for many years,
And I'd pray you'd be there to erase my fears.

Missing You

I miss you each and every day,
Each time the sun shines my way.
In the morning, when I rise,
I visualize your face in the skies.
Where you are, I wish to be,
But I prefer you here with me.
I'll follow the big and bright star,
Taking me there where you are.
Until I see your face again,
I'll be missing you now and then.
So I'm saving for you all my love,
As I search for the brightest star above.

No One Knows

No one knows the magic of your charms,
And the electrifying touch of your arms.
You send chills throughout my soul,
There is so much that is untold.

The magic you possess is so unique,
It will never fade for me to seek.
At times you give a precious rose,
To keep me dancing on my toes.

You manage to stay deep in my mind,
And share great thoughts all the time.
These are only a few great things you do,
That keep me so head over heels with you.

Take the Time to Express Yourself

At times we must set aside,
A moment for you and I.
To express the love that abides,
Within our hearts as days go by.
To show how much we appreciate,
The many things we've shared.
While other times we may procrastinate,
On expressing how much we care.
Therefore, I'm taking the time to let you know,
That you're my strength and my inspiration.
And to remind you that I love you so,
And this is stated without hesitation.

My Request

As I rest my aching feet,
And close my eyes to fall asleep.
Please grant to me a peaceful night,
Filled with stars that shine so bright.
I ask that you will smile on me,
Another day I hope to see.
But if it's time to move on,
Please welcome me into your home.
And if my loved ones shed a tear,
Please remind them that you are near.
To comfort them, and pull them through,
Dear Lord, this is my request to you.

Lord, I Need Your Help

If I am weak, please strengthen me,
To be as strong as you desire me to be.
I need my strength to perform,
And to help others who may mourn.

If I am sad, please lift my spirit,
I cannot perform if I am weary.
I want to enjoy this life of mine,
If I go wrong, please give me a sign.

If I'm flying too high, please bring me down,
A little bit closer toward the ground.
And if I'm too low, please lift me up,
I want to be worthy of your holy cup.

If I shall travel the darkest path,
Please give me light that will last.
And if by chance I cannot see,
Please guide my steps, I ask of thee.

If I shall wonder and go astray,
Turn me around and show me the way.
And if I am lost, please lead me home,
Lord, stay by my side so I will not roam.

God is always there to assist you
In everything that you do.

A Prayer of Understanding

I really hate to be a bother,
But I need some understanding, Father.
I find it hard to comprehend,
Why some people refuse to bend.
Some are determined to do things their way,
And say whatever they choose to say.
Regardless of whether it's right or wrong,
They think it's a crime to bite their tongues.
They have no respect for the feelings of others,
And some go as far as disrespecting their mothers.
Father touch their hearts, so they may see,
A better person, they should be.

What God Will Do for You

God will wake you every morning,
And help you out of bed.
And if you have a headache,
He'll ease your aching head.
He'll help you in the bathroom,
For you to take a bath.
He's so great and wonderful,
The best friend you'll ever have.
God will gladly assist you,
In preparing your daily meals.
There's no fees for His service,
So He will never leave a bill.
He'll walk you to the door,
Each day you go to work.
He'll be there by your side,
To help you stay alert.
God will be your chauffeur,
As you drive alone.
He will never leave you,
To make it on your own.
He'll spend the entire day,
Right there by your side.
All you'll need to do,
Is relax and enjoy the ride.

Just Me, Myself, and I

As I strolled through the park, just me, myself, and I,
Many thoughts came to mind.
I decided to take a detour and turn left.
While walking down the street, thinking to myself.
With many thoughts running through my head,
These are the words to myself I said.
How blessed am I this day to see,
Myself replied and said to me.
I enjoy the sun shining oh so bright,
And the peace I feel throughout the night.
I took a deep breath of fresh air,
And continued walking without a care.
Suddenly, I said to myself,
"I am blessed to have so much energy left."

It is okay to talk to yourself.

God versus Satan

Satan smiles when you are down,
God eliminates all your frowns.
Satan walks away, and encourages evil,
God stays by your side, and never leaves you.
Satan rejoices when you are sad,
God comforts you and smiles when you're glad.
Satan will try to destroy your happy home,
God builds it up with a pleasant tone.
Satan presents a heavy load,
But God leads you to a smoother road.
Satan will grant you so many tears,
God protects you from all fears.
Satan guides you to sinking sand,
God has a solid rock for you to stand.
Satan's work will soon be concealed,
But God's work will always reveal.

Satan offers a world of temptation.
God gives eternal salvation!

Reach for His Hand

If times get hard and friends are few,
And you feel as though there's nothing left to do.
Just stretch out your arms as far as you can,
And reach for God's almighty hand.
If your burdens are hard to bear,
Turn to God; He's always there.
You'll find you have a friend above,
To shower you with all His love.
When Satan tries to bring you down,
Stop and take a look around.
You'll see that God's been good to you,
And He will always carry you through.
Just take a look, and there He'll stand,
And reach for God's unchanging hand.

Satan is busy,
But God does more.

Join Me in Prayer

Come join me in a word of prayer,
And relieve your worries, if you dare.
Prayers will ease your troubles away,
And give you peace throughout the day.

Come join me as I kneel and say,
Lord, in your Son's name, we humbly pray.
For eternal life that never ends;
Your passion I beg for you to send.

We'll feel the power of His love,
Surrounding us from above.
Join me in prayer, I ask of you,
We'll have peace the whole day through.

A Prayer of Thanks

I thank you, Lord, for loving me,
You are so sweet and kind.
Because of you, I am free,
And have a peace of mind.
I come to you in times of need,
You lend a helping hand.
A friend to me, you are indeed,
Always willing to take a stand.

A Good Deed

Today you did a tremendous deed,
By assisting Floyd, who was in need.
But throughout the remaining of the day,
You bragged of your support in every way.
Your good deed was immediately destroyed,
Because you boasted about helping Floyd.

Don't destroy your blessing.

My Lord, My Lord

My Lord, my Lord, I love you so,
Wherever you send me, I will go.
I'll cherish this life you've given me,
In your mansion, one day I hope to be.

My Lord, my Lord, on you I call,
When Satan causes me to fall.
Your caring ways and loving touch,
Cause me to depend on you so much.

You're always available when I'm in need
And never fail to take the lead.
Never once have you hesitated,
Because of this, I am so elated.

My Lord, my Lord, I need your love,
To shine on me from above.
There's not a day that's gone by,
You did not hear my humble cry.

As I Travel

As I travel through this world of sin,
I'll carry your love deep within.
It comforts me when I'm in need,
It is the greatest, yes indeed.

As I travel this earthly path,
I must always remain steadfast.
Keeping in mind, I have a goal,
To reach out and touch a lost soul.

As I travel from place to place,
I'll know my journey is not a waste.
We'll always walk hand in hand,
I'll forever be your greatest fan.

The Power of His Love

Feel the power of His love,
And the joy from above.

Feel the power from deep within,
A broken heart it shall mend.

Feel the power as you speak,
Eternal bliss you shall seek.

Have Mercy, Lord

Lord, I pray for your mercy every day,
And forgiveness as I journey along the way.
If I shall fall, please lift me,
And mold me to be who you want me to be.

Have mercy, Lord, and forgive my sins,
This I ask of you once again.
Guide me through this sinful world,
As I graciously give my life a twirl.

Have mercy on me, my dear Lord,
Without you, my life is a void.
Have mercy, Lord, hear my plea,
This I humbly beg of thee.

Have mercy, Lord, on me today,
Please guide me so I will not stray.
I need for you to save my soul,
And for you to make me whole.
God is a merciful God.

God Is the Way

God is truly the only way,
On Him I depend every day.
Dear Lord, my Savior is all I need,

Improved, my life has been indeed.
Since the day I found my Lord,

Temptation, I must continue to avoid.
He is the greatest of them all,
Every day, on Him I call.

Worldly goods, I need not possess,
All I need is my Lord, I do confess.
Yes, God is the way.

Staying on the Right Track

While strolling the road to eternal bliss,
Satan will try to turn me around.
I must continue marching forward,
And not allow him to bring me down.

Tempting me with his worldly goods,
As he tries to block my pathway.
I must keep him at a distance,
And not allow myself to stray.

I must move forward, staying on the right track,
I cannot afford to think of turning back.
Until I reach my destiny,
I must move forward patiently.

As Children of God

As children of God, we must stand tall,
And God is there in case we shall fall.
Stumbling blocks will come our way,
Yet God will guide us every day.
And if by chance we shall stumble,
We must trust in God and be humble.
We'll reap the joy God has for us,
And all the blessings; that's a plus!

God will certainly make us whole.
He'll brighten our days and strengthen our souls.

Satan Will Try to Hold You Back

As you walk the path of righteousness,
Satan will try to turn you around.
Keep on stepping and praying for the Lord,
To keep your feet on solid grounds.

Obstacles will come to hold you back.
But trust in God, He'll keep you on the right track.
He'll lead you around them every day,
And clear the path along the way.

Don't allow Satan to hold you back.

God's Word

God's Word is my weapon. It's my sword and shield,
It's locked in my mind and is forever sealed.
It's my protection from all earthly temptation,
And will lend the way to eternal salvation.

God's Word is medication to make me whole,
It heals within my body and soul.
It gives me strength when I'm in need,
And helps me to sow a very good seed.

God's Word is the solution to a restless night,
It never vanishes, but always in sight.
It's there when I need consolation,
All it takes is a little meditation.

God's Word is forever so divine,
And is available to all mankind.
It's just like a convenience store,
That keeps me coming back for more.

God Is All of That

God is everything you'll ever hope for,
With Him in your life, you cannot ask for more.
He'll be your friend and your guide,
He'll always make certain you're satisfied.

He'll be your father and your mother,
He'll also be your sister and brother.
God is all of that and then some more,
He's always there to open a door.

He'll be your water when you need a drink,
He'll close your eyes if you need to blink.
God is everything you need Him to be,
He'll be your fruit hanging on a tree.

God is the wind that often blows,
He'll be your heat when you are cold.
He is your shelter during a storm,
He'll lift your spirit, if you shall mourn.

God is your lamp when you need a light,
He'll be with you throughout the night.
God is all that, and so much more,
And your needs, He'll never ignore.

Let the Past Remain in the Past

Let the past remain in the past,
And focus on future endeavors.
Don't keep dwelling on what has happened,
Instead, concentrate on what *can* happen.
Whatever was done yesterday cannot be erased,
So keep moving on to the next phase.

Complain, Complain, Complain

You get up in the morning, and what do you do?
Complain, complain, complain.

You walk around the whole day through,
Complain, complain, complain.

The only words in your vocabulary is,
Complain, complain, complain.

Don't waste your time
Complaining about things you have no control over.

Change Your Evil Ways

When I was hot,
You turned up the heat.
When I was standing,
You refused to offer a seat.

When I needed a ride home,
You refused to take me there.
When I was cold,
You turned on the air.

When I was hospitalized,
Your visit, I did lack.
When I opened the door,
You chose to shut it back.

When I asked for your help,
You always turned me down.
When I gave a smile,
You walked away and frowned.

When I walked through the door,
You stuck out your feet.
Your life of cruelty,
God will defeat.

Teach Me, Lord

Lord, teach me how to pray,
I want to feel your presence every day.
Teach me how to be so humble,
And how not to moan and crumble.

Lord teach me how to stay strong,
In your Word and not go wrong.
Teach me how to never fear,
Because you are forever near.

Nutritious Thoughts

If the stars refuse to shine,
Take a moment to unwind.
And you will see in due time,
You shall have a restful mind.

The Extra Mile

I'll worship God when He wants me to,
Because every day will be like new.

I'll do whatever He asks of me,
And remain obedient as can be.

I'll climb a mountain, if that's what it takes,
To be near my Lord; I won't hesitate.

I'll swim across the widest sea,
If that's the way it has to be.

And if He says stay and do not go,
I'll stay seated because He said so.

I will go the extra mile for my Lord
Until I achieve my reward.

I Have Found a Savior

I've found my Redeemer who is everything to me,
He is my foundation and my solid rock.
I've opened the door to let Him in,
Because I heard His eager knock.

I've found a Savior, and I'm very proud,
He will never leave me, He is always there.
He has never turned His back,
But shows how much He cares.

I have found my Savior,
And He will never forsake me.
He is the greatest,
And He will not deceive me.

I Have Been Blessed

Lord, you've blessed me with a beautiful day,
This is something I can never repay.
You've always blessed me to see the light,
And the stars shining throughout the night.
You've been my shelter during a storm,
And throughout the cold days, you kept me warm.
When I needed to breathe, you were a breath of fresh air,
And when I needed a friend, you were always there.
You held my hand when I was afraid,
My debt to you, Lord, could never be paid.

Call on Jesus

If your friends have all gone,
And you feel so alone.
Call on Jesus, He's just a phone call away,
And He will certainly brighten your day.

If you are feeling sad and blue,
Jesus will bring happiness to you.
Just call on Him, and He'll be there,
No matter when, why, or where.

He's always there for you.

Jesus, Jesus, Jesus

Jesus, Jesus, Jesus,
How great it is to call your name.
Jesus, Jesus, Jesus,
I will never feel ashamed.
Jesus, Jesus, Jesus,
You are my dear precious friend.
Jesus, Jesus, Jesus,
I'll say it over and over again.

Jesus, Jesus, Jesus,
You are the greatest of them all.
Jesus, Jesus, Jesus,
You gave me the capacity to stand tall.
Jesus, Jesus, Jesus,
My whole life depends on you.
Jesus, Jesus, Jesus,
Our friendship binds like glue.

Jesus, Jesus, Jesus,
What a great advocate.
Jesus, Jesus, Jesus,
Satan is just the opposite.
Jesus, Jesus, Jesus,
On your name I'll always call.
Jesus, Jesus, Jesus,
You deserve a loud applause.

Jesus, Jesus, Jesus,
Your work is so amazing.
Jesus, Jesus, Jesus,
It's you that I am praising.
Jesus, Jesus, Jesus,
You are my solid rock.
Jesus, Jesus, Jesus,
You've accepted me on your dock.

Never be afraid to call His name.

There Is No Need to Cry

There's no need for you to cry,
Those miserable days have all gone by.
God is showering you with His blessings,
And is teaching you various lessons.
He is blessing you in so many ways,
And is awarding you with sunny days.
He's giving you comfort during your times of need,
He is the greatest, your necessities He will feed.

It's Always Someone Else's Fault

Whenever things seem to go wrong,
It's always someone else's fault.

Whenever you're late for work each day,
It's someone else's fault.

Whenever you tell a lie,
It's someone else's fault.

Whenever you can't sleep at night,
It's someone else's fault.

Whenever you fail to handle your responsibilities,
It's someone else's fault.

Whenever your life falls apart,
It's someone else's fault.

Take responsibility for your own actions!

Same Old Tune

You sit around all day long,
Singing that same old sad song.
Why don't you try a different tune,
Or park yourself in another room.
Because that tune is getting old,
This is something you should be told.
A pleasant tune won't hurt sometimes,
You are driving me out of my mind.
Everything gets old some day,
So find another tune to play.

God Is There Throughout the Season

God does not need a reason,
To do good throughout the season.
But if you're feeling all alone,
He'll send His angels to surround your home.
To accompany you along the way,
Bringing to you a joyous day.
If your days are cloudy and blue,
He'll brighten them up just for you.
And if by chance you are in tears,
He'll give you a smile that can last for years.

Nutritious Thoughts

Take the time to smell the roses,
And the freshness in the air.
Take the time to relax,
And ease your mind without a care.

God's Mansion

There is a mansion waiting for me,
When I reach my final destiny.
It is prepared for you as well,
A permanent home for us to dwell.
In this mansion we'll never feel weary,
And the days are never dreary.
So get prepared, it doesn't cost a dime,
We'll meet our loved ones, and have a great time.
My dad will welcome me with a smile,
Saying, "Come on in, my dear child."
My cousins will be waiting for me,
I'll visit my in-laws, most definitely.
I will certainly pay my uncles a visit
Around the throne where they may sit.
Eventually, God will bring my dear mother,
We'll celebrate with my sister and brother.
My children and grandchildren will come in due time,
We'll join together as we dine.
My friends and siblings will be there some day,
In this mansion, we all shall stay.

Personal Poem

In Dedication to Dad, Sister Betty, and Brother Eugene

Our dearly beloved sister, brother, and dad,
We will always treasure those moments we've had.
Thoughts of you linger throughout the years,
Sometimes we may even shed a few tears.
Your spirit is with us and will never disappear,
And in our hearts, you will forever be near.
We'll always think of you, and cherish those memories,
Occasionally, we may imagine your face in sceneries.
You will forever hold a special place in our hearts,
And our love for you will never, ever part.

We love and miss you!

During Your Darkest Hours

God is always there for you,
He will certainly pull you through.
Taking all your pain away,
And granting to you a brighter day.
He will wash away your sorrows,
Awarding you with a brighter tomorrow.
Just trust in Him and believe,
He will place your mind at ease.